MznLnx

Missing Links Exam Preps

Exam Prep for

Product Design and Development

Ulrich & Eppinger, 4th Edition

The MznLnx Exam Prep is your link from the texbook and lecture to your exams.
The MznLnx Exam Preps are unauthorized and comprehensive reviews of your textbooks.

All material provided by MznLnx and Rico Publications (c) 2010
Textbook publishers and textbook authors do not particpate in or contribute to these reviews.

MznLnx

Rico
Publications

Exam Prep for Product Design and Development
4th Edition
Ulrich & Eppinger

Publisher: Raymond Houge
Assistant Editor: Michael Rouger
Text and Cover Designer: Lisa Buckner
Marketing Manager: Sara Swagger
Project Manager, Editorial Production: Jerry Emerson
Art Director: Vernon Lowerui

Product Manager: Dave Mason
Editorial Assitant: Rachel Guzmanji
Pedagogy: Debra Long
Cover Image: Jim Reed/Getty Images
Text and Cover Printer: City Printing, Inc.
Compositor: Media Mix, Inc.

(c) 2010 Rico Publications
ALL RIGHTS RESERVED. No part of this work covered by the copyright may be reproduced or used in any form or by an means--graphic, electronic, or mechanical, including photocopying, recording, taping, Web distribution, information storage, and retrieval systems, or in any other manner--without the written permission of the publisher.

For more information about our products, contact us at:
Dave.Mason@RicoPublications.com

For permission to use material from this text or product, submit a request online to:
Dave.Mason@RicoPublications.com

Printed in the United States
ISBN:

Contents

CHAPTER 1
Introduction — 1

CHAPTER 2
Development Processes and Organizations — 4

CHAPTER 3
Product Planning — 9

CHAPTER 4
Identifying Customer Needs — 15

CHAPTER 5
Product Specifications — 19

CHAPTER 6
Concept Generation — 25

CHAPTER 7
Concept Selection — 29

CHAPTER 8
Concept Testing — 31

CHAPTER 9
Product Architecture — 35

CHAPTER 10
Industrial Design — 38

CHAPTER 11
Design for Manufacturing — 42

CHAPTER 12
Prototyping — 47

CHAPTER 13
Robust Design — 49

CHAPTER 14
Patents and Intellectual Property — 53

CHAPTER 15
Product Development Economics — 58

CHAPTER 16
Managing Projects — 63

ANSWER KEY — 68

TO THE STUDENT

COMPREHENSIVE

The *MznLnx* Exam Prep series is designed to help you pass your exams. Editors at MznLnx review your textbooks and then prepare these practice exams to help you master the textbook material. Unlike study guides, workbooks, and practice tests provided by the texbook publisher and textbook authors, *MznLnx* gives you **all** of the material in each chapter in exam form, not just samples, so you can be sure to nail your exam.

MECHANICAL

The MznLnx Exam Prep series creates exams that will help you learn the subject matter as well as test you on your understanding. Each question is designed to help you master the concept. Just working through the exams, you gain an understanding of the subject--its a simple mechanical process that produces success.

INTEGRATED STUDY GUIDE AND REVIEW

MznLnx is not just a set of exams designed to test you, its also a comprehensive review of the subject content. Each exam question is also a review of the concept, making sure that you will get the answer correct without having to go to other sources of material. You learn as you go! Its the easiest way to pass an exam.

HUMOR

Studying can be tedious and dry. MznLnx's instructional design includes moderate humor within the exam questions on occassion, to break the tedium and revitalize the brain

Chapter 1. Introduction

1. In economics, business, retail, and accounting, a _____ is the value of money that has been used up to produce something, and hence is not available for use anymore. In economics, a _____ is an alternative that is given up as a result of a decision. In business, the _____ may be one of acquisition, in which case the amount of money expended to acquire it is counted as _____.
    a. Transaction cost
    b. Cost
    c. Fixed costs
    d. Variable cost

2. In business and engineering, new _____ is the term used to describe the complete process of bringing a new product or service to market. There are two parallel paths involved in the Nproduct development process: one involves the idea generation, product design, and detail engineering; the other involves market research and marketing analysis. Companies typically see new _____ as the first stage in generating and commercializing new products within the overall strategic process of product life cycle management used to maintain or grow their market share.
    a. New product screening
    b. Product development
    c. New product development
    d. Specification tree

3. _____ is defined by the American _____ Association as the activity, set of institutions, and processes for creating, communicating, delivering, and exchanging offerings that have value for customers, clients, partners, and society at large. The term developed from the original meaning which referred literally to going to market, as in shopping, or going to a market to sell goods or services.

    _____ practice tends to be seen as a creative industry, which includes advertising, distribution and selling.

    a. Marketing myopia
    b. Product naming
    c. Customer acquisition management
    d. Marketing

4. A _____ or logistics network is the system of organizations, people, technology, activities, information and resources involved in moving a product or service from supplier to customer. _____ activities transform natural resources, raw materials and components into a finished product that is delivered to the end customer. In sophisticated _____ systems, used products may re-enter the _____ at any point where residual value is recyclable.
    a. Purchasing
    b. Supply chain
    c. Supply chain network
    d. Demand chain management

Chapter 1. Introduction

5. A _____ is a list of the general tasks and responsibilities of a position. Typically, it also includes to whom the position reports, specifications such as the qualifications needed by the person in the job, salary range for the position, etc. A _____ is usually developed by conducting a job analysis, which includes examining the tasks and sequences of tasks necessary to perform the job.
   a. Job description
   b. Power III
   c. 6-3-5 Brainwriting
   d. 180SearchAssistant

6. In economics, _____ are business expenses that are not dependent on the activities of the business They tend to be time-related, such as salaries or rents being paid per month. This is in contrast to variable costs, which are volume-related (and are paid per quantity.)

   In management accounting, _____ are defined as expenses that do not change in proportion to the activity of a business, within the relevant period or scale of production.

   a. Variable cost
   b. Marginal cost
   c. Transaction cost
   d. Fixed costs

7. _____s is the social science that studies the production, distribution, and consumption of goods and services. The term _____s comes from the Ancient Greek οἰκονομία from οἶκος (oikos, 'house') + νόμος (nomos, 'custom' or 'law'), hence 'rules of the house(hold)'. Current _____ models developed out of the broader field of political economy in the late 19th century, owing to a desire to use an empirical approach more akin to the physical sciences.
   a. Industrial organization
   b. Economic
   c. ADTECH
   d. ACNielsen

8. Human beings are also considered to be _____ because they have the ability to change raw materials into valuable _____. The term Human _____ can also be defined as the skills, energies, talents, abilities and knowledge that are used for the production of goods or the rendering of services. While taking into account human beings as _____, the following things have to be kept in mind:

   - The size of the population
   - The capabilities of the individuals in that population

   Many _____ cannot be consumed in their original form. They have to be processed in order to change them into more usable commodities.

Chapter 1. Introduction

a. Power III
b. 6-3-5 Brainwriting
c. Resources
d. 180SearchAssistant

Chapter 2. Development Processes and Organizations

1. _____ in organizations and public policy is both the organizational process of creating and maintaining a plan; and the psychological process of thinking about the activities required to create a desired goal on some scale. As such, it is a fundamental property of intelligent behavior. This thought process is essential to the creation and refinement of a plan, or integration of it with other plans, that is, it combines forecasting of developments with the preparation of scenarios of how to react to them.
   a. 6-3-5 Brainwriting
   b. Planning
   c. Power III
   d. 180SearchAssistant

2. In business and engineering, new _____ is the term used to describe the complete process of bringing a new product or service to market. There are two parallel paths involved in the Nproduct development process: one involves the idea generation, product design, and detail engineering; the other involves market research and marketing analysis. Companies typically see new _____ as the first stage in generating and commercializing new products within the overall strategic process of product life cycle management used to maintain or grow their market share.
   a. Product development
   b. Specification tree
   c. New product development
   d. New product screening

3. _____ refers to planned and systematic production processes that provide confidence in a product's suitability for its intended purpose. Refer to the definition by Merriam-Webster for further information . It is a set of activities intended to ensure that products (goods and/or services) satisfy customer requirements in a systematic, reliable fashion.
   a. 180SearchAssistant
   b. 6-3-5 Brainwriting
   c. Power III
   d. Quality assurance

4. Proof-of-Principle _____ This type of _____ is used to test some aspect of the intended design without attempting to exactly simulate the visual appearance, choice of materials or intended manufacturing process. Such _____s can be used to 'prove' out a potential design approach such as range of motion, mechanics, sensors, architecture, etc.
   a. Power III
   b. Prototype
   c. 6-3-5 Brainwriting
   d. 180SearchAssistant

5. A _____ is an explicit set of requirements to be satisfied by a material, product, or service.

Chapter 2. Development Processes and Organizations

In engineering, manufacturing, and business, it is vital for suppliers, purchasers, and users of materials, products, or services to understand and agree upon all requirements. A _____ is a type of a standard which is often referenced by a contract or procurement document.

   a. New product development
   b. Product optimization
   c. Product development
   d. Specification

6. _____ is the process of comparing the cost, cycle time, productivity, or quality of a specific process or method to another that is widely considered to be an industry standard or best practice. The result is often a business case for making changes in order to make improvements. The term _____ was first used by cobblers to measure ones feet for shoes.
   a. Strategic group
   b. Switching cost
   c. Business strategy
   d. Benchmarking

7. _____ is the process of using quantitative methods and qualitative methods to evaluate consumer response to a product idea prior to the introduction of a product to the market. It can also be used to generate communication designed to alter consumer attitudes toward existing products. These methods involve the evaluation by consumers of product concepts having certain rational benefits, such as 'a detergent that removes stains but is gentle on fabrics,' or non-rational benefits, such as 'a shampoo that lets you be yourself.' Such methods are commonly referred to as _____ and have been performed using field surveys, personal interviews and focus groups, in combination with various quantitative methods, to generate and evaluate product concepts.
   a. Logit analysis
   b. Cross tabulation
   c. Market analysis
   d. Concept testing

8. _____s is the social science that studies the production, distribution, and consumption of goods and services. The term _____s comes from the Ancient Greek οἰκονομία from οἶκος (oikos, 'house') + νόμος (nomos, 'custom' or 'law'), hence 'rules of the house(hold)'. Current _____ models developed out of the broader field of political economy in the late 19th century, owing to a desire to use an empirical approach more akin to the physical sciences.
   a. Economic
   b. Industrial organization
   c. ACNielsen
   d. ADTECH

Chapter 2. Development Processes and Organizations

9. _____ is part of project management, which relates to the use of schedules such as Gantt charts to plan and subsequently report progress within the project environment.

Initially, the project scope is defined and the appropriate methods for completing the project are determined. Following this step, the durations for the various tasks necessary to complete the work are listed and grouped into a work breakdown structure.

a. Project planning
b. Power III
c. Product breakdown structure
d. 180SearchAssistant

10. _____ is a concept that denotes the precise probability of specific eventualities. Technically, the notion of _____ is independent from the notion of value and, as such, eventualities may have both beneficial and adverse consequences. However, in general usage the convention is to focus only on potential negative impact to some characteristic of value that may arise from a future event.

a. Risk
b. Power III
c. 6-3-5 Brainwriting
d. 180SearchAssistant

11. _____ is a measure of the strength of a brand, product, service relative to competitive offerings. There is often a geographic element to the competitive landscape. In defining _____, you must see to what extent a product, brand, or firm controls a product category in a given geographic area.

a. Productivity
b. Discretionary spending
c. Market dominance
d. Market system

12. In statistics, an _____ is a term in a statistical model added when the effect of two or more variables is not simply additive. Such a term reflects that the effect of one variable depends on the values of one or more other variables.

Thus, for a response Y and two variables x_1 and x_2 an additive model would be:

$$Y = ax_1 + bx_2 + \text{error}$$

Chapter 2. Development Processes and Organizations

In contrast to this,

$$Y = ax_1 + bx_2 + c(x_1 \times x_2) + \text{error},$$

is an example of a model with an _____ between variables x_1 and x_2 ('error' refers to the random variable whose value by which y differs from the expected value of y.)

a. ADTECH
b. ACNielsen
c. AMAX
d. Interaction

13. _____ is the practice of individuals including commercial businesses, governments and institutions, facilitating the sale of their products or services to other companies or organizations that in turn resell them, use them as components in products or services they offer _____ is also called business-to-_____ for short. (Note that while marketing to government entities shares some of the same dynamics of organizational marketing, B2G Marketing is meaningfully different.)
    a. Disruptive technology
    b. Business marketing
    c. Law of disruption
    d. Mass marketing

14. A _____ is a list of the general tasks and responsibilities of a position. Typically, it also includes to whom the position reports, specifications such as the qualifications needed by the person in the job, salary range for the position, etc. A _____ is usually developed by conducting a job analysis, which includes examining the tasks and sequences of tasks necessary to perform the job.
    a. 180SearchAssistant
    b. Power III
    c. 6-3-5 Brainwriting
    d. Job description

15. A _____ is a type of bar chart that illustrates a project schedule. A _____ illustrates the start and finish dates of the terminal elements and summary elements of a project. Terminal elements and summary elements comprise the work breakdown structure of the project.

Chapter 2. Development Processes and Organizations

    a. Gantt chart
    b. Power III
    c. 6-3-5 Brainwriting
    d. 180SearchAssistant

16. In finance, an _____ is a contract between a buyer and a seller that gives the buyer the right--but not the obligation--to buy or to sell a particular asset (the underlying asset) at a later day at an agreed price. In return for granting the _____, the seller collects a payment (the premium) from the buyer. A call _____ gives the buyer the right to buy the underlying asset; a put _____ gives the buyer of the _____ the right to sell the underlying asset.
    a. ADTECH
    b. ACNielsen
    c. AMAX
    d. Option

Chapter 3. Product Planning

1. _____ is the ongoing process of identifying and articulating market requirements that define a product's feature set.
   a. Brand parity
   b. Targeted advertising
   c. Market intelligence
   d. Product planning

2. _____ is a global document management company which manufactures and sells a range of color and black-and-white printers, multifunction systems, photo copiers, digital production printing presses, and related consulting services and supplies. Xerox is headquartered in Norwalk, Connecticut , though its largest population of employees is based in and around Rochester, New York, the area in which the company was founded. The Xerox 914 was the first one-piece plain paper photocopier, and sold in the thousands.

   Xerox was founded in 1906 in Rochester, New York as 'The Haloid Company', which originally manufactured photographic paper and equipment.

   a. Japan Advertising Photographers' Association
   b. Partnership for a Drug-Free America
   c. Xerox Corporation
   d. Green Earth Market

3. _____ in organizations and public policy is both the organizational process of creating and maintaining a plan; and the psychological process of thinking about the activities required to create a desired goal on some scale. As such, it is a fundamental property of intelligent behavior. This thought process is essential to the creation and refinement of a plan, or integration of it with other plans, that is, it combines forecasting of developments with the preparation of scenarios of how to react to them.
   a. 180SearchAssistant
   b. 6-3-5 Brainwriting
   c. Planning
   d. Power III

4. A _____ is a plan of action designed to achieve a particular goal.

   _____ is different from tactics. In military terms, tactics is concerned with the conduct of an engagement while _____ is concerned with how different engagements are linked.

a. 6-3-5 Brainwriting
b. Power III
c. 180SearchAssistant
d. Strategy

5. In business and engineering, new _____ is the term used to describe the complete process of bringing a new product or service to market. There are two parallel paths involved in the Nproduct development process: one involves the idea generation, product design, and detail engineering; the other involves market research and marketing analysis. Companies typically see new _____ as the first stage in generating and commercializing new products within the overall strategic process of product life cycle management used to maintain or grow their market share.
   a. Product development
   b. Specification tree
   c. New product screening
   d. New product development

6. Competitiveness is a comparative concept of the ability and performance of a firm, sub-sector or country to sell and supply goods and/or services in a given market. Although widely used in economics and business management, the usefulness of the concept, particularly in the context of national competitiveness, is vigorously disputed by economists, such as Paul Krugman.

The term may also be applied to markets, where it is used to refer to the extent to which the market structure may be regarded as perfectly _____.

   a. Geographical pricing
   b. Customs union
   c. Free trade zone
   d. Competitive

7. In economics, business, retail, and accounting, a _____ is the value of money that has been used up to produce something, and hence is not available for use anymore. In economics, a _____ is an alternative that is given up as a result of a decision. In business, the _____ may be one of acquisition, in which case the amount of money expended to acquire it is counted as _____.
   a. Fixed costs
   b. Transaction cost
   c. Variable cost
   d. Cost

Chapter 3. Product Planning

8. _____ is a concept developed by Michael Porter, used in business strategy. It describes a way to establish the competitive advantage. _____, in basic words, means the lowest cost of operation in the industry.
   a. Cost leadership
   b. Corporate strategy
   c. Chaotics
   d. Strategic group

9. In finance, an _____ is a contract between a buyer and a seller that gives the buyer the right--but not the obligation--to buy or to sell a particular asset (the underlying asset) at a later day at an agreed price. In return for granting the _____, the seller collects a payment (the premium) from the buyer. A call _____ gives the buyer the right to buy the underlying asset; a put _____ gives the buyer of the _____ the right to sell the underlying asset.
   a. AMAX
   b. ADTECH
   c. ACNielsen
   d. Option

10. A _____ is a subgroup of people or organizations sharing one or more characteristics that cause them to have similar product and/or service needs. A true _____ meets all of the following criteria: it is distinct from other segments (different segments have different needs), it is homogeneous within the segment (exhibits common needs); it responds similarly to a market stimulus, and it can be reached by a market intervention. The term is also used when consumers with identical product and/or service needs are divided up into groups so they can be charged different amounts.
    a. Production orientation
    b. Customer insight
    c. Commercial planning
    d. Market segment

11. _____ is a term used by project managers and project management (PM) organizations to describe methods for analyzing and collectively managing a group of current or proposed projects based on numerous key characteristics. The fundamental objective of the _____ process is to determine the optimal mix and sequencing of proposed projects to best achieve the organization's overall goals - typically expressed in terms of hard economic measures, business strategy goals, or technical strategy goals - while honoring constraints imposed by management or external real-world factors. Typical attributes of projects being analyzed in a _____ process include each project's total expected cost, consumption of scarce resources (human or otherwise) expected timeline and schedule of investment, expected nature, magnitude and timing of benefits to be realized, and relationship or inter-dependencies with other projects in the portfolio.
    a. Customer intelligence
    b. Project Portfolio Management
    c. Power III
    d. Pop-up ads

Chapter 3. Product Planning

12. Human beings are also considered to be _____ because they have the ability to change raw materials into valuable _____. The term Human _____ can also be defined as the skills, energies, talents, abilities and knowledge that are used for the production of goods or the rendering of services. While taking into account human beings as _____, the following things have to be kept in mind:

    - The size of the population
    - The capabilities of the individuals in that population

Many _____ cannot be consumed in their original form. They have to be processed in order to change them into more usable commodities.

   a. 6-3-5 Brainwriting
   b. 180SearchAssistant
   c. Resources
   d. Power III

13. _____ is a rivalry between individuals, groups, nations for territory, a niche, or allocation of resources. It arises whenever two or more parties strive for a goal which cannot be shared. _____ occurs naturally between living organisms which co-exist in the same environment.
   a. Price fixing
   b. Competition
   c. Non-price competition
   d. Price competition

14. A _____ is a group of employees from various functional areas of the organization - research, engineering, marketing, finance. human resources, and operations, for example - who are all focused on a specific objective and are responsible to work as a team to improve coordination and innovation across divisions and resolve mutual problems.
   a. Job analysis
   b. Power III
   c. 180SearchAssistant
   d. Cross-functional team

15. A _____ is a brief statement of the purpose of a company, organization. It is ideally used to guide the actions of the organization.

_____s often contain the following:

- Purpose of the organization
- The organization's primary stakeholders: clients, stockholders, etc.
- Responsibilities of the organization towards these stockholders
- Products and services offered

Generally shorter _____s are more effective than longer ones.

In developing a _____:

- Encourage input as feasible from employees, volunteers, and other stakeholders
- Publicize it broadly

The _____ can be used to resolve differences between business stakeholders. Stakeholders include: employees including managers and executives, stockholders, board of directors, customers, suppliers, distributors, creditors, governments (local, state, federal, etc.), unions, competitors, NGO's, and the general public.

a. 180SearchAssistant
b. 6-3-5 Brainwriting
c. Power III
d. Mission statement

16. _____ is the provision of service to customers before, during and after a purchase.

According to Turban et al., '_____ is a series of activities designed to enhance the level of customer satisfaction - that is, the feeling that a product or service has met the customer expectation.'

Its importance varies by product, industry and customer.

a. COPC Inc.
b. Customer experience
c. Customer service
d. Facing

17. _____ is an advertisement in which a particular product specifically mentions a competitor by name for the express purpose of showing why the competitor is inferior to the product naming it.

This should not be confused with parody advertisements, where a fictional product is being advertised for the purpose of poking fun at the particular advertisement, nor should it be confused with the use of a coined brand name for the purpose of comparing the product without actually naming an actual competitor. ('Wikipedia tastes better and is less filling than the Encyclopedia Galactica.')

In the 1980s, during what has been referred to as the cola wars, soft-drink manufacturer Pepsi ran a series of advertisements where people, caught on hidden camera, in a blind taste test, chose Pepsi over rival Coca-Cola.

   a. Comparative advertising
   b. Heavy-up
   c. GI-70
   d. Cost per conversion

18. _____ is systematic determination of merit, worth, and significance of something or someone using criteria against a set of standards. _____ often is used to characterize and appraise subjects of interest in a wide range of human enterprises, including the arts, criminal justice, foundations and non-profit organizations, government, health care, and other human services.

Depending on the topic of interest, there are professional groups which look to the quality and rigor of the _____ process.

   a. ADTECH
   b. AMAX
   c. Evaluation
   d. ACNielsen

Chapter 4. Identifying Customer Needs

1. In business and engineering, new _____ is the term used to describe the complete process of bringing a new product or service to market. There are two parallel paths involved in the Nproduct development process: one involves the idea generation, product design, and detail engineering; the other involves market research and marketing analysis. Companies typically see new _____ as the first stage in generating and commercializing new products within the overall strategic process of product life cycle management used to maintain or grow their market share.

   a. New product development
   b. Specification tree
   c. New product screening
   d. Product development

2. A _____ is a brief statement of the purpose of a company, organization. It is ideally used to guide the actions of the organization.

   _____s often contain the following:

   - Purpose of the organization
   - The organization's primary stakeholders: clients, stockholders, etc.
   - Responsibilities of the organization towards these stockholders
   - Products and services offered

   Generally shorter _____s are more effective than longer ones.

   In developing a _____:

   - Encourage input as feasible from employees, volunteers, and other stakeholders
   - Publicize it broadly

   The _____ can be used to resolve differences between business stakeholders. Stakeholders include: employees including managers and executives, stockholders, board of directors, customers, suppliers, distributors, creditors, governments (local, state, federal, etc.), unions, competitors, NGO's, and the general public.

   a. 6-3-5 Brainwriting
   b. 180SearchAssistant
   c. Power III
   d. Mission statement

3. A _____ is an explicit set of requirements to be satisfied by a material, product, or service.

   In engineering, manufacturing, and business, it is vital for suppliers, purchasers, and users of materials, products, or services to understand and agree upon all requirements. A _____ is a type of a standard which is often referenced by a contract or procurement document.

Chapter 4. Identifying Customer Needs

a. New product development
b. Specification
c. Product optimization
d. Product development

4. _____ refer to a collection of facts usually collected as the result of experience, observation or experiment or a set of premises. This may consist of numbers, words particularly as measurements or observations of a set of variables. _____ are often viewed as a lowest level of abstraction from which information and knowledge are derived.

a. Pearson product-moment correlation coefficient
b. Sample size
c. Mean
d. Data

5. _____ is a term used to describe a process of preparing and collecting data - for example as part of a process improvement or similar project.

_____ usually takes place early on in an improvement project, and is often formalised through a _____ Plan which often contains the following activity.

1. Pre collection activity - Agree goals, target data, definitions, methods
2. Collection - _____
3. Present Findings - usually involves some form of sorting analysis and/or presentation.

A formal _____ process is necessary as it ensures that data gathered is both defined and accurate and that subsequent decisions based on arguments embodied in the findings are valid . The process provides both a baseline from which to measure from and in certain cases a target on what to improve. Types of _____ 1-By mail questionnaires 2-By personal interview

- Six sigma
- Sampling (statistics)

a. 180SearchAssistant
b. 6-3-5 Brainwriting
c. Power III
d. Data collection

6. _____ is a term for unprocessed data, it is also known as primary data. It is a relative term _____ can be input to a computer program or used in manual analysis procedures such as gathering statistics from a survey.

Chapter 4. Identifying Customer Needs

   a. Chief marketing officer
   b. Shoppers Food ' Pharmacy
   c. Raw data
   d. Product manager

7. A _____ is a form of qualitative research in which a group of people are asked about their attitude towards a product, service, concept, advertisement, idea, or packaging. Questions are asked in an interactive group setting where participants are free to talk with other group members.

Ernest Dichter originated the idea of having a 'group therapy' for products and this process is what became known as a _____.

   a. Cross tabulation
   b. Logit analysis
   c. Focus group
   d. Marketing research process

8. _____ is either an activity of a living being (such as a human), consisting of receiving knowledge of the outside world through the senses, or the recording of data using scientific instruments. The term may also refer to any datum collected during this activity.

The scientific method requires _____s of nature to formulate and test hypotheses.

   a. AMAX
   b. ACNielsen
   c. ADTECH
   d. Observation

9. _____ is a term developed by Eric von Hippel in 1986. His definition for _____ is:

   1. _____s face needs that will be general in a marketplace - but face them months or years before the bulk of that marketplace encounters them, and
   2. _____s are positioned to benefit significantly by obtaining a solution to those needs.

In other words: _____s are users of a product that currently experience needs still unknown to the public and who also benefit greatly if they obtain a solution to these needs.

Chapter 4. Identifying Customer Needs

The _____ Method is a market research tool that may be used by companies and / or individuals seeking to develop breakthrough products. _____ methodology was originally developed by Dr. Eric von Hippel of the Massachusetts Institute of Technology (MIT) and first described in the July 1986 issue of the Journal of Management Science.

a. 6-3-5 Brainwriting
b. Lead user
c. Power III
d. 180SearchAssistant

10. _____ is the process of comparing the cost, cycle time, productivity, or quality of a specific process or method to another that is widely considered to be an industry standard or best practice. The result is often a business case for making changes in order to make improvements. The term _____ was first used by cobblers to measure ones feet for shoes.

a. Strategic group
b. Business strategy
c. Switching cost
d. Benchmarking

11. In statistics, an _____ is a term in a statistical model added when the effect of two or more variables is not simply additive. Such a term reflects that the effect of one variable depends on the values of one or more other variables.

Thus, for a response Y and two variables x_1 and x_2 an additive model would be:

$$Y = ax_1 + bx_2 + \text{error}$$

In contrast to this,

$$Y = ax_1 + bx_2 + c(x_1 \times x_2) + \text{error},$$

is an example of a model with an _____ between variables x_1 and x_2 ('error' refers to the random variable whose value by which y differs from the expected value of y.)

a. AMAX
b. ADTECH
c. ACNielsen
d. Interaction

Chapter 5. Product Specifications

1. A _____ is an explicit set of requirements to be satisfied by a material, product, or service.

In engineering, manufacturing, and business, it is vital for suppliers, purchasers, and users of materials, products, or services to understand and agree upon all requirements. A _____ is a type of a standard which is often referenced by a contract or procurement document.

   a. Product development
   b. New product development
   c. Product optimization
   d. Specification

2. _____ is a 'method to transform user demands into design quality, to deploy the functions forming quality, and to deploy methods for achieving the design quality into subsystems and component parts, and ultimately to specific elements of the manufacturing process.', as described by Dr. Yoji Akao, who originally developed _____ in Japan in 1966, when the author combined his work in quality assurance and quality control points with function deployment used in Value Engineering.

_____ is designed to help planners focus on characteristics of a new or existing product or service from the viewpoints of market segments, company, or technology-development needs. The technique yields graphs and matrices.

   a. Quality Function Deployment
   b. Power III
   c. 180SearchAssistant
   d. Futurist

3. The terms '_____' and 'independent variable' are used in similar but subtly different ways in mathematics and statistics as part of the standard terminology in those subjects. They are used to distinguish between two types of quantities being considered, separating them into those available at the start of a process and those being created by it, where the latter (_____s) are dependent on the former (independent variables.)

In traditional calculus, a function is defined as a relation between two terms called variables because their values vary.

   a. Power III
   b. Dependent variable
   c. Field experiment
   d. 180SearchAssistant

Chapter 5. Product Specifications

4. _____s are used in open sentences. For instance, in the formula x + 1 = 5, x is a _____ which represents an 'unknown' number. _____s are often represented by letters of the Roman alphabet, or those of other alphabets, such as Greek, and use other special symbols.
   a. Personalization
   b. Quantitative
   c. Book of business
   d. Variable

5. _____ is a broad label that refers to any individuals or households that use goods and services generated within the economy. The concept of a _____ is used in different contexts, so that the usage and significance of the term may vary.

A _____ is a person who uses any product or service.

   a. Power III
   b. Consumer
   c. 6-3-5 Brainwriting
   d. 180SearchAssistant

6. _____ is an American magazine published monthly by Consumers Union. It publishes reviews and comparisons of consumer products and services based on reporting and results from its in-house testing laboratory. It also publishes cleaning and general buying guides.
   a. Power III
   b. Magalog
   c. Consumer Reports
   d. Crossing the Chasm

7. A _____ is the space, actual or metaphorical, in which a market operates. The term is also used in a trademark law context to denote the actual consumer environment, ie. the 'real world' in which products and services are provided and consumed.
   a. 180SearchAssistant
   b. Power III
   c. 6-3-5 Brainwriting
   d. Marketplace

Chapter 5. Product Specifications

8. In business and engineering, new _____ is the term used to describe the complete process of bringing a new product or service to market. There are two parallel paths involved in the Nproduct development process: one involves the idea generation, product design, and detail engineering; the other involves market research and marketing analysis. Companies typically see new _____ as the first stage in generating and commercializing new products within the overall strategic process of product life cycle management used to maintain or grow their market share.
   a. Product development
   b. New product development
   c. New product screening
   d. Specification tree

9. _____ is systematic determination of merit, worth, and significance of something or someone using criteria against a set of standards. _____ often is used to characterize and appraise subjects of interest in a wide range of human enterprises, including the arts, criminal justice, foundations and non-profit organizations, government, health care, and other human services.

Depending on the topic of interest, there are professional groups which look to the quality and rigor of the _____ process.

   a. ADTECH
   b. Evaluation
   c. AMAX
   d. ACNielsen

10. _____ is the process of comparing the cost, cycle time, productivity, or quality of a specific process or method to another that is widely considered to be an industry standard or best practice. The result is often a business case for making changes in order to make improvements. The term _____ was first used by cobblers to measure ones feet for shoes.
    a. Switching cost
    b. Business strategy
    c. Strategic group
    d. Benchmarking

11. _____ is an applied art whereby the aesthetics and usability of mass-produced products may be improved for marketability and production. The role of an _____er is to create and execute design solutions towards problems of form, usability, user ergonomics, engineering, marketing, brand development and sales.

The term '_____' is often attributed to the designer Joseph Claude Sinel in 1919 (although he himself denied it in later interviews) but the discipline predates that by at least a decade.

Chapter 5. Product Specifications

a. Albert Einstein
b. African Americans
c. AStore
d. Industrial design

12. A personal and cultural _____ is a relative ethic _____, an assumption upon which implementation can be extrapolated. A _____ system is a set of consistent _____s and measures that is soo not true. A principle _____ is a foundation upon which other _____s and measures of integrity are based.
   a. Perceptual maps
   b. Supreme Court of the United States
   c. Package-on-Package
   d. Value

13. Proof-of-Principle _____ This type of _____ is used to test some aspect of the intended design without attempting to exactly simulate the visual appearance, choice of materials or intended manufacturing process. Such _____s can be used to 'prove' out a potential design approach such as range of motion, mechanics, sensors, architecture, etc.
   a. 6-3-5 Brainwriting
   b. Power III
   c. 180SearchAssistant
   d. Prototype

14. In economics, business, retail, and accounting, a _____ is the value of money that has been used up to produce something, and hence is not available for use anymore. In economics, a _____ is an alternative that is given up as a result of a decision. In business, the _____ may be one of acquisition, in which case the amount of money expended to acquire it is counted as _____.
   a. Transaction cost
   b. Fixed costs
   c. Variable cost
   d. Cost

15. _____ is a pricing method used by firms. It is defined as 'a cost management tool for reducing the overall cost of a product over its entire life-cycle with the help of production, engineering, research and design'. _____ finds the maximum amount of cost that can be incurred on a product and with it the firm can still earn the required profit margin from that product at a particular selling price.

Chapter 5. Product Specifications

a. Target costing
b. Competitor indexing
c. Premium pricing
d. Fee

16. _____s is the social science that studies the production, distribution, and consumption of goods and services. The term _____s comes from the Ancient Greek oá¼°κονομῑα from oá¼¶κος (oikos, 'house') + vÏŒμος (nomos, 'custom' or 'law'), hence 'rules of the house(hold)'. Current _____ models developed out of the broader field of political economy in the late 19th century, owing to a desire to use an empirical approach more akin to the physical sciences.

a. ADTECH
b. Economic
c. ACNielsen
d. Industrial organization

17. Competitiveness is a comparative concept of the ability and performance of a firm, sub-sector or country to sell and supply goods and/or services in a given market. Although widely used in economics and business management, the usefulness of the concept, particularly in the context of national competitiveness, is vigorously disputed by economists, such as Paul Krugman .

The term may also be applied to markets, where it is used to refer to the extent to which the market structure may be regarded as perfectly _____.

a. Customs union
b. Free trade zone
c. Competitive
d. Geographical pricing

18. _____ is a statistical technique used in market research to determine how people value different features that make up an individual product or service.

The objective of _____ is to determine what combination of a limited number of attributes is most influential on respondent choice or decision making. A controlled set of potential products or services is shown to respondents and by analyzing how they make preferences between these products, the implicit valuation of the individual elements making up the product or service can be determined.

a. Likert scale
b. Power III
c. Semantic differential
d. Conjoint analysis

19. _____ generally refers to a list of all planned expenses and revenues. It is a plan for saving and spending. A _____ is an important concept in microeconomics, which uses a _____ line to illustrate the trade-offs between two or more goods.
   a. 6-3-5 Brainwriting
   b. Budget
   c. Power III
   d. 180SearchAssistant

20. _____ is a pricing method used by companies. It is used primarily because it is easy to calculate and requires little information. There are several varieties, but the common thread in all of them is that one first calculates the cost of the product, then includes an additional amount to represent profit.
   a. Relationship based pricing
   b. Break even analysis
   c. Loss leader
   d. Cost-plus pricing

21. _____ is one of the four Ps of the marketing mix. The other three aspects are product, promotion, and place. It is also a key variable in microeconomic price allocation theory.
   a. Competitor indexing
   b. Price
   c. Relationship based pricing
   d. Pricing

Chapter 6. Concept Generation

1. In business and engineering, new _____ is the term used to describe the complete process of bringing a new product or service to market. There are two parallel paths involved in the Nproduct development process: one involves the idea generation, product design, and detail engineering; the other involves market research and marketing analysis. Companies typically see new _____ as the first stage in generating and commercializing new products within the overall strategic process of product life cycle management used to maintain or grow their market share.
   a. New product screening
   b. Product development
   c. Specification tree
   d. New product development

2. _____ refers to the process by which tissues of dead organisms break down into simpler forms of matter. Such a breakdown of dead organisms is essential for new growth and development of living organisms because it recycles the finite chemical constituents and frees up the limited physical space in the biome. Bodies of living organisms begin to decompose shortly after death.
   a. 180SearchAssistant
   b. 6-3-5 Brainwriting
   c. Power III
   d. Decomposition

3. In economics, an externality or spillover of an economic transaction is an impact on a party that is not directly involved in the transaction. In such a case, prices do not reflect the full costs or benefits in production or consumption of a product or service. A positive impact is called an _____ benefit, while a negative impact is called an _____ cost.
   a. ADTECH
   b. ACNielsen
   c. AMAX
   d. External

4. _____ is a term developed by Eric von Hippel in 1986. His definition for _____ is:

   1. _____s face needs that will be general in a marketplace - but face them months or years before the bulk of that marketplace encounters them, and
   2. _____s are positioned to benefit significantly by obtaining a solution to those needs.

In other words: _____s are users of a product that currently experience needs still unknown to the public and who also benefit greatly if they obtain a solution to these needs.

The _____ Method is a market research tool that may be used by companies and / or individuals seeking to develop breakthrough products. _____ methodology was originally developed by Dr. Eric von Hippel of the Massachusetts Institute of Technology (MIT) and first described in the July 1986 issue of the Journal of Management Science.

Chapter 6. Concept Generation

   a. 180SearchAssistant
   b. Power III
   c. Lead user
   d. 6-3-5 Brainwriting

5. _____ is the process of comparing the cost, cycle time, productivity, or quality of a specific process or method to another that is widely considered to be an industry standard or best practice. The result is often a business case for making changes in order to make improvements. The term _____ was first used by cobblers to measure ones feet for shoes.
   a. Business strategy
   b. Switching cost
   c. Strategic group
   d. Benchmarking

6. A _____ is a set of exclusive rights granted by a State to an inventor or his assignee for a limited period of time in exchange for a disclosure of an invention.

The procedure for granting _____s, the requirements placed on the _____ee and the extent of the exclusive rights vary widely between countries according to national laws and international agreements. Typically, however, a _____ application must include one or more claims defining the invention which must be new, inventive, and useful or industrially applicable.

   a. Foreign Corrupt Practices Act
   b. Product liability
   c. Reasonable person standard
   d. Patent

7. A _____ or trade mark, identified by the symbols ™ (not yet registered) and ® (registered) business organization or other legal entity to identify that the products and/or services to consumers with which the _____ appears originate from a unique source of origin, and to distinguish its products or services from those of other entities. A _____ is a type of intellectual property, and typically a name, word, phrase, logo, symbol, design, image, or a combination of these elements. There is also a range of non-conventional _____s comprising marks which do not fall into these standard categories.
   a. Trademark
   b. Power III
   c. Risk management
   d. 180SearchAssistant

8. The _____ is an agency in the United States Department of Commerce that issues patents to inventors and businesses for their inventions, and trademark registration for product and intellectual property identification.

Chapter 6. Concept Generation 27

The USPTO is currently based in Alexandria, Virginia, after a 2006 move from the Crystal City area of Arlington, Virginia. The offices under Patents and the Chief Information Officer that remained just outside the southern end of Crystal City completed moving to Randolph Square, a brand new building in Shirlington Village, on 27 April 2009.

   a. United States Patent and Trademark Office
   b. INVISTA
   c. Underwriters Laboratories
   d. Access Commerce

9. A _____ is a type of wholesale merchant business that buys goods and bulk products from importers, other wholesalers and then sells to retailers. _____s can deal in any commodity destined for the retail market. Typical categories are food, lumber, hardware, fuel, and textiles.
   a. Refusal to deal
   b. Chief privacy officer
   c. Tacit collusion
   d. Jobbing house

10. The _____ of American Manufacturers is a multi-volume directory of industrial product information covering 650,000 distributors, manufacturers and service companies within 67,000-plus industrial categories. It was first published in 1898 by Harvey Mark Thomas as Hardware and Kindred Trades. The company stopped publishing its print products in 2006 due to declining circulation as Internet searches eroded the products' usability.
   a. Stock management
   b. Free box
   c. Futura plus
   d. Thomas Register

11. A _____ attribute is one that exists in a range of magnitudes, and can therefore be measured. Measurements of any particular _____ property are expressed as a specific quantity, referred to as a unit, multiplied by a number. Examples of physical quantities are distance, mass, and time.
   a. Dolly Dimples
   b. Lifestyle city
   c. BeyondROI
   d. Quantitative

Chapter 6. Concept Generation

12. _____ is systematic determination of merit, worth, and significance of something or someone using criteria against a set of standards. _____ often is used to characterize and appraise subjects of interest in a wide range of human enterprises, including the arts, criminal justice, foundations and non-profit organizations, government, health care, and other human services.

Depending on the topic of interest, there are professional groups which look to the quality and rigor of the _____ process.

a. Evaluation
b. AMAX
c. ACNielsen
d. ADTECH

Chapter 7. Concept Selection

1. In business and engineering, new _____ is the term used to describe the complete process of bringing a new product or service to market. There are two parallel paths involved in the Nproduct development process: one involves the idea generation, product design, and detail engineering; the other involves market research and marketing analysis. Companies typically see new _____ as the first stage in generating and commercializing new products within the overall strategic process of product life cycle management used to maintain or grow their market share.

   a. New product development
   b. Specification tree
   c. Product development
   d. New product screening

2. In economics, an externality or spillover of an economic transaction is an impact on a party that is not directly involved in the transaction. In such a case, prices do not reflect the full costs or benefits in production or consumption of a product or service. A positive impact is called an _____ benefit, while a negative impact is called an _____ cost.

   a. ADTECH
   b. External
   c. ACNielsen
   d. AMAX

3. Competitiveness is a comparative concept of the ability and performance of a firm, sub-sector or country to sell and supply goods and/or services in a given market. Although widely used in economics and business management, the usefulness of the concept, particularly in the context of national competitiveness, is vigorously disputed by economists, such as Paul Krugman.

   The term may also be applied to markets, where it is used to refer to the extent to which the market structure may be regarded as perfectly _____.

   a. Geographical pricing
   b. Competitive
   c. Free trade zone
   d. Customs union

4. _____ is the process of comparing the cost, cycle time, productivity, or quality of a specific process or method to another that is widely considered to be an industry standard or best practice. The result is often a business case for making changes in order to make improvements. The term _____ was first used by cobblers to measure ones feet for shoes.

   a. Business strategy
   b. Benchmarking
   c. Switching cost
   d. Strategic group

Chapter 7. Concept Selection

5. _____ can be regarded as an outcome of mental processes (cognitive process) leading to the selection of a course of action among several alternatives. Every _____ process produces a final choice. The output can be an action or an opinion of choice.
   a. Power III
   b. Decision making
   c. 6-3-5 Brainwriting
   d. 180SearchAssistant

6. _____ is systematic determination of merit, worth, and significance of something or someone using criteria against a set of standards. _____ often is used to characterize and appraise subjects of interest in a wide range of human enterprises, including the arts, criminal justice, foundations and non-profit organizations, government, health care, and other human services.

Depending on the topic of interest, there are professional groups which look to the quality and rigor of the _____ process.

   a. Evaluation
   b. ADTECH
   c. AMAX
   d. ACNielsen

7. _____ refers to the process by which tissues of dead organisms break down into simpler forms of matter. Such a breakdown of dead organisms is essential for new growth and development of living organisms because it recycles the finite chemical constituents and frees up the limited physical space in the biome. Bodies of living organisms begin to decompose shortly after death.
   a. 6-3-5 Brainwriting
   b. Decomposition
   c. Power III
   d. 180SearchAssistant

8. In economics, business, retail, and accounting, a _____ is the value of money that has been used up to produce something, and hence is not available for use anymore. In economics, a _____ is an alternative that is given up as a result of a decision. In business, the _____ may be one of acquisition, in which case the amount of money expended to acquire it is counted as _____.
   a. Transaction cost
   b. Variable cost
   c. Cost
   d. Fixed costs

Chapter 8. Concept Testing

1. _____ is the process of using quantitative methods and qualitative methods to evaluate consumer response to a product idea prior to the introduction of a product to the market. It can also be used to generate communication designed to alter consumer attitudes toward existing products. These methods involve the evaluation by consumers of product concepts having certain rational benefits, such as 'a detergent that removes stains but is gentle on fabrics,' or non-rational benefits, such as 'a shampoo that lets you be yourself.' Such methods are commonly referred to as _____ and have been performed using field surveys, personal interviews and focus groups, in combination with various quantitative methods, to generate and evaluate product concepts.
   a. Concept testing
   b. Logit analysis
   c. Cross tabulation
   d. Market analysis

2. A _____ is an advance video or DVD copy of a film sent to critics, awards voters, video stores (for their manager and employees), and other film industry professionals, including producers and distributors. Often, each individual _____ is sent out with distinct markings (such as a digital watermark), which allow copies of a _____ to be tracked to their source.

In 2003 the MPAA announced that they would be ceasing distribution of _____s to Academy members, citing fears of piracy.

   a. Madrid system
   b. Screener
   c. Geographical indication
   d. Trademark dilution

3. In statistics, an _____ is a term in a statistical model added when the effect of two or more variables is not simply additive. Such a term reflects that the effect of one variable depends on the values of one or more other variables.

Thus, for a response Y and two variables x_1 and x_2 an additive model would be:

$$Y = ax_1 + bx_2 + \text{error}$$

In contrast to this,

$$Y = ax_1 + bx_2 + c(x_1 \times x_2) + \text{error},$$

is an example of a model with an _____ between variables x_1 and x_2 ('error' refers to the random variable whose value by which y differs from the expected value of y.)

Chapter 8. Concept Testing

a. Interaction
b. ADTECH
c. AMAX
d. ACNielsen

4. _____ is a standard point of view or personal prejudice. especially when the tendency interferes with the ability to be impartial, unprejudiced, or objective. The term _____ed is used to describe an action, judgment, or other outcome influenced by a prejudged perspective.

a. 180SearchAssistant
b. Power III
c. 6-3-5 Brainwriting
d. Bias

5. _____ is the imitation of some real thing, state of affairs, or process. The act of simulating something generally entails representing certain key characteristics or behaviors of a selected physical or abstract system.

_____ is used in many contexts, including the modeling of natural systems or human systems in order to gain insight into their functioning.

a. 6-3-5 Brainwriting
b. 180SearchAssistant
c. Power III
d. Simulation

6. In the mathematical discipline of graph theory a _____ or edge-independent set in a graph is a set of edges without common vertices. It may also be an entire graph consisting of edges without common vertices.

Given a graph G = (V,E), a _____ M in G is a set of pairwise non-adjacent edges; that is, no two edges share a common vertex.

a. Power III
b. Matching
c. 6-3-5 Brainwriting
d. 180SearchAssistant

Chapter 8. Concept Testing

7. Proof-of-Principle _____ This type of _____ is used to test some aspect of the intended design without attempting to exactly simulate the visual appearance, choice of materials or intended manufacturing process. Such _____s can be used to 'prove' out a potential design approach such as range of motion, mechanics, sensors, architecture, etc.
   a. 180SearchAssistant
   b. 6-3-5 Brainwriting
   c. Power III
   d. Prototype

8. _____ is a broad label that refers to any individuals or households that use goods and services generated within the economy. The concept of a _____ is used in different contexts, so that the usage and significance of the term may vary.

   A _____ is a person who uses any product or service.

   a. 6-3-5 Brainwriting
   b. Power III
   c. 180SearchAssistant
   d. Consumer

9. In business and engineering, new _____ is the term used to describe the complete process of bringing a new product or service to market. There are two parallel paths involved in the Nproduct development process: one involves the idea generation, product design, and detail engineering; the other involves market research and marketing analysis. Companies typically see new _____ as the first stage in generating and commercializing new products within the overall strategic process of product life cycle management used to maintain or grow their market share.
   a. Specification tree
   b. New product screening
   c. New product development
   d. Product development

10. _____ is the process of estimation in unknown situations. Prediction is a similar, but more general term. Both can refer to estimation of time series, cross-sectional or longitudinal data.
    a. 180SearchAssistant
    b. Power III
    c. 6-3-5 Brainwriting
    d. Forecasting

Chapter 8. Concept Testing

11. _____ is one of the four Ps of the marketing mix. The other three aspects are product, promotion, and place. It is also a key variable in microeconomic price allocation theory.
    a. Price
    b. Pricing
    c. Competitor indexing
    d. Relationship based pricing

12. _____ involves disseminating information about a product, product line, brand, or company. It is one of the four key aspects of the marketing mix. (The other three elements are product marketing, pricing, and distribution). P>_____ is generally sub-divided into two parts:

    - Above the line _____: Promotion in the media (e.g. TV, radio, newspapers, Internet and Mobile Phones) in which the advertiser pays an advertising agency to place the ad
    - Below the line _____: All other _____. Much of this is intended to be subtle enough for the consumer to be unaware that _____ is taking place. E.g. sponsorship, product placement, endorsements, sales _____, merchandising, direct mail, personal selling, public relations, trade shows

    a. Bottling lines
    b. Promotion
    c. Cashmere Agency
    d. Davie Brown Index

13. _____s are used in open sentences. For instance, in the formula x + 1 = 5, x is a _____ which represents an 'unknown' number. _____s are often represented by letters of the Roman alphabet, or those of other alphabets, such as Greek, and use other special symbols.
    a. Book of business
    b. Personalization
    c. Quantitative
    d. Variable

Chapter 9. Product Architecture

1. In business and engineering, new _____ is the term used to describe the complete process of bringing a new product or service to market. There are two parallel paths involved in the Nproduct development process: one involves the idea generation, product design, and detail engineering; the other involves market research and marketing analysis. Companies typically see new _____ as the first stage in generating and commercializing new products within the overall strategic process of product life cycle management used to maintain or grow their market share.
   a. New product screening
   b. Specification tree
   c. New product development
   d. Product development

2. In economics, business, retail, and accounting, a _____ is the value of money that has been used up to produce something, and hence is not available for use anymore. In economics, a _____ is an alternative that is given up as a result of a decision. In business, the _____ may be one of acquisition, in which case the amount of money expended to acquire it is counted as _____.
   a. Fixed costs
   b. Variable cost
   c. Cost
   d. Transaction cost

3. A _____ is a group of employees from various functional areas of the organization - research, engineering, marketing, finance, human resources, and operations, for example - who are all focused on a specific objective and are responsible to work as a team to improve coordination and innovation across divisions and resolve mutual problems.
   a. Power III
   b. 180SearchAssistant
   c. Job analysis
   d. Cross-functional team

4. A _____ is a plan of action designed to achieve a particular goal.

   _____ is different from tactics. In military terms, tactics is concerned with the conduct of an engagement while _____ is concerned with how different engagements are linked.

   a. Power III
   b. 180SearchAssistant
   c. 6-3-5 Brainwriting
   d. Strategy

5. In statistics, an _____ is a term in a statistical model added when the effect of two or more variables is not simply additive. Such a term reflects that the effect of one variable depends on the values of one or more other variables.

Thus, for a response Y and two variables x_1 and x_2 an additive model would be:

$$Y = ax_1 + bx_2 + \text{error}$$

In contrast to this,

$$Y = ax_1 + bx_2 + c(x_1 \times x_2) + \text{error},$$

is an example of a model with an _____ between variables x_1 and x_2 ('error' refers to the random variable whose value by which y differs from the expected value of y.)

a. AMAX
b. ACNielsen
c. ADTECH
d. Interaction

6. A _____ or logistics network is the system of organizations, people, technology, activities, information and resources involved in moving a product or service from supplier to customer. _____ activities transform natural resources, raw materials and components into a finished product that is delivered to the end customer. In sophisticated _____ systems, used products may re-enter the _____ at any point where residual value is recyclable.
   a. Purchasing
   b. Demand chain management
   c. Supply chain network
   d. Supply chain

7. A _____ is a subgroup of people or organizations sharing one or more characteristics that cause them to have similar product and/or service needs. A true _____ meets all of the following criteria: it is distinct from other segments (different segments have different needs), it is homogeneous within the segment (exhibits common needs); it responds similarly to a market stimulus, and it can be reached by a market intervention. The term is also used when consumers with identical product and/or service needs are divided up into groups so they can be charged different amounts.
   a. Customer insight
   b. Production orientation
   c. Commercial planning
   d. Market segment

Chapter 9. Product Architecture

8. _____ in organizations and public policy is both the organizational process of creating and maintaining a plan; and the psychological process of thinking about the activities required to create a desired goal on some scale. As such, it is a fundamental property of intelligent behavior. This thought process is essential to the creation and refinement of a plan, or integration of it with other plans, that is, it combines forecasting of developments with the preparation of scenarios of how to react to them.

   a. 6-3-5 Brainwriting
   b. Power III
   c. 180SearchAssistant
   d. Planning

9. A _____ is an explicit set of requirements to be satisfied by a material, product, or service.

In engineering, manufacturing, and business, it is vital for suppliers, purchasers, and users of materials, products, or services to understand and agree upon all requirements. A _____ is a type of a standard which is often referenced by a contract or procurement document.

   a. New product development
   b. Product optimization
   c. Specification
   d. Product development

Chapter 10. Industrial Design

1. _____ is an applied art whereby the aesthetics and usability of mass-produced products may be improved for marketability and production. The role of an _____er is to create and execute design solutions towards problems of form, usability, user ergonomics, engineering, marketing, brand development and sales.

The term '_____' is often attributed to the designer Joseph Claude Sinel in 1919 (although he himself denied it in later interviews) but the discipline predates that by at least a decade.

   a. Industrial design
   b. African Americans
   c. Albert Einstein
   d. AStore

2. In economics, business, retail, and accounting, a _____ is the value of money that has been used up to produce something, and hence is not available for use anymore. In economics, a _____ is an alternative that is given up as a result of a decision. In business, the _____ may be one of acquisition, in which case the amount of money expended to acquire it is counted as _____.
   a. Transaction cost
   b. Variable cost
   c. Fixed costs
   d. Cost

3. In business and engineering, new _____ is the term used to describe the complete process of bringing a new product or service to market. There are two parallel paths involved in the Nproduct development process: one involves the idea generation, product design, and detail engineering; the other involves market research and marketing analysis. Companies typically see new _____ as the first stage in generating and commercializing new products within the overall strategic process of product life cycle management used to maintain or grow their market share.
   a. New product development
   b. New product screening
   c. Product development
   d. Specification tree

4. In economics, _____ is a measure of the relative satisfaction from consumption of various goods and services. Given this measure, one may speak meaningfully of increasing or decreasing _____, and thereby explain economic behavior in terms of attempts to increase one's _____. For illustrative purposes, changes in _____ are sometimes expressed in units called utils.
   a. ADTECH
   b. ACNielsen
   c. AMAX
   d. Utility

Chapter 10. Industrial Design

5. In statistics, an _____ is a term in a statistical model added when the effect of two or more variables is not simply additive. Such a term reflects that the effect of one variable depends on the values of one or more other variables.

Thus, for a response Y and two variables x_1 and x_2 an additive model would be:

$$Y = ax_1 + bx_2 + \text{error}$$

In contrast to this,

$$Y = ax_1 + bx_2 + c(x_1 \times x_2) + \text{error},$$

is an example of a model with an _____ between variables x_1 and x_2 ('error' refers to the random variable whose value by which y differs from the expected value of y.)

a. AMAX
b. ADTECH
c. Interaction
d. ACNielsen

6. _____ is the set of reasons that determines one to engage in a particular behavior. The term is generally used for human _____ but, theoretically, it can be used to describe the causes for animal behavior as well

a. Motivation
b. Role playing
c. 180SearchAssistant
d. Power III

7. _____ is the state or fact of exclusive rights and control over property, which may be an object, land/real estate, or some other kind of property (like government-granted monopolies collectively referred to as intellectual property.) It is embodied in an _____ right also referred to as title.

_____ is the key building block in the development of the capitalist socio-economic system.

a. ADTECH
b. AMAX
c. ACNielsen
d. Ownership

8. A _____ is a set of exclusive rights granted by a State to an inventor or his assignee for a limited period of time in exchange for a disclosure of an invention.

The procedure for granting _____s, the requirements placed on the _____ee and the extent of the exclusive rights vary widely between countries according to national laws and international agreements. Typically, however, a _____ application must include one or more claims defining the invention which must be new, inventive, and useful or industrially applicable.

   a. Product liability
   b. Reasonable person standard
   c. Foreign Corrupt Practices Act
   d. Patent

9. In marketing, a _____ is the 'persona' of a corporation which is designed to accord with and facilitate the attainment of business objectives. It is usually visibly manifested by way of branding and the use of trademarks.

_____ comes into being when there is a common ownership of an organisational philosophy that is manifest in a distinct corporate culture -- the corporate personality.

   a. Brand orientation
   b. Corporate identity
   c. Brand recognition
   d. Brand ambassador

10. _____ is a measure of the strength of a brand, product, service relative to competitive offerings. There is often a geographic element to the competitive landscape. In defining _____, you must see to what extent a product, brand, or firm controls a product category in a given geographic area.
   a. Market system
   b. Discretionary spending
   c. Productivity
   d. Market dominance

11. Proof-of-Principle _____ This type of _____ is used to test some aspect of the intended design without attempting to exactly simulate the visual appearance, choice of materials or intended manufacturing process. Such _____s can be used to 'prove' out a potential design approach such as range of motion, mechanics, sensors, architecture, etc.
   a. 6-3-5 Brainwriting
   b. 180SearchAssistant
   c. Power III
   d. Prototype

Chapter 10. Industrial Design

12. _____ is the automatic construction of physical objects using solid freeform fabrication. The first techniques for _____ became available in the late 1980s and were used to produce models and prototype parts. Today, they are used for a much wider range of applications and are even used to manufacture production quality parts in relatively small numbers.

   a. Product management
   b. Service life
   c. Product lifecycle
   d. Rapid prototyping

13. Human beings are also considered to be _____ because they have the ability to change raw materials into valuable _____. The term Human _____ can also be defined as the skills, energies, talents, abilities and knowledge that are used for the production of goods or the rendering of services. While taking into account human beings as _____, the following things have to be kept in mind:

   - The size of the population
   - The capabilities of the individuals in that population

Many _____ cannot be consumed in their original form. They have to be processed in order to change them into more usable commodities.

   a. 6-3-5 Brainwriting
   b. Power III
   c. Resources
   d. 180SearchAssistant

14. In marketing, _____ is the process of distinguishing the differences of a product or offering from others, to make it more attractive to a particular target market. This involves differentiating it from competitors' products as well as one's own product offerings.

Differentiation is a source of competitive advantage.

   a. Packshot
   b. Marketing myopia
   c. Corporate image
   d. Product differentiation

Chapter 11. Design for Manufacturing

1. A _____ is a group of employees from various functional areas of the organization - research, engineering, marketing, finance. human resources, and operations, for example - who are all focused on a specific objective and are responsible to work as a team to improve coordination and innovation across divisions and resolve mutual problems.
   a. Power III
   b. 180SearchAssistant
   c. Job analysis
   d. Cross-functional team

2. In economics, business, retail, and accounting, a _____ is the value of money that has been used up to produce something, and hence is not available for use anymore. In economics, a _____ is an alternative that is given up as a result of a decision. In business, the _____ may be one of acquisition, in which case the amount of money expended to acquire it is counted as _____.
   a. Transaction cost
   b. Fixed costs
   c. Cost
   d. Variable cost

3. In business and engineering, new _____ is the term used to describe the complete process of bringing a new product or service to market. There are two parallel paths involved in the Nproduct development process: one involves the idea generation, product design, and detail engineering; the other involves market research and marketing analysis. Companies typically see new _____ as the first stage in generating and commercializing new products within the overall strategic process of product life cycle management used to maintain or grow their market share.
   a. New product screening
   b. Product development
   c. New product development
   d. Specification tree

4. In economics, _____ are business expenses that are not dependent on the activities of the business They tend to be time-related, such as salaries or rents being paid per month. This is in contrast to variable costs, which are volume-related (and are paid per quantity.)

   In management accounting, _____ are defined as expenses that do not change in proportion to the activity of a business, within the relevant period or scale of production.

   a. Marginal cost
   b. Variable cost
   c. Transaction cost
   d. Fixed costs

Chapter 11. Design for Manufacturing

5. _____s are used in open sentences. For instance, in the formula x + 1 = 5, x is a _____ which represents an 'unknown' number. _____s are often represented by letters of the Roman alphabet, or those of other alphabets, such as Greek, and use other special symbols.
   a. Quantitative
   b. Variable
   c. Personalization
   d. Book of business

6. _____s are expenses that change in proportion to the activity of a business. In other words, _____ is the sum of marginal costs. It can also be considered normal costs.
   a. Fixed costs
   b. Marginal cost
   c. Transaction cost
   d. Variable cost

7. In accounting, _____ has a very specific meaning. It is an outflow of cash or other valuable assets from a person or company to another person or company. This outflow of cash is generally one side of a trade for products or services that have equal or better current or future value to the buyer than to the seller.
   a. AMAX
   b. ACNielsen
   c. ADTECH
   d. Expense

8. A _____ is a type of wholesale merchant business that buys goods and bulk products from importers, other wholesalers and then sells to retailers. _____s can deal in any commodity destined for the retail market. Typical categories are food, lumber, hardware, fuel, and textiles.
   a. Chief privacy officer
   b. Tacit collusion
   c. Refusal to deal
   d. Jobbing house

9. A _____ is something that is acted upon or used by or by human labour or industry, for use as a building material to create some product or structure. Often the term is used to denote material that came from nature and is in an unprocessed or minimally processed state. Iron ore, logs, and crude oil, would be examples.

Chapter 11. Design for Manufacturing

    a. Power III
    b. 6-3-5 Brainwriting
    c. Raw material
    d. 180SearchAssistant

10. The _____ of American Manufacturers is a multi-volume directory of industrial product information covering 650,000 distributors, manufacturers and service companies within 67,000-plus industrial categories. It was first published in 1898 by Harvey Mark Thomas as Hardware and Kindred Trades. The company stopped publishing its print products in 2006 due to declining circulation as Internet searches eroded the products' usability.
    a. Stock management
    b. Free box
    c. Futura plus
    d. Thomas Register

11. _____ is a costing model that identifies activities in an organization and assigns the cost of each activity resource to all products and services according to the actual consumption by each: it assigns more indirect costs (overhead) into direct costs.

In this way an organization can establish the true cost of its individual products and services for the purposes of identifying and eliminating those which are unprofitable and lowering the prices of those which are overpriced.

In a business organization, the ABC methodology assigns an organization's resource costs through activities to the products and services provided to its customers.

    a. ACNielsen
    b. Activity-based costing
    c. ADTECH
    d. AMAX

12. _____, in microeconomics, are the cost advantages that a business obtains due to expansion. They are factors that cause a producer's average cost per unit to fall as output rises. Diseconomies of scale are the opposite.
    a. ADTECH
    b. AMAX
    c. ACNielsen
    d. Economies of scale

Chapter 11. Design for Manufacturing

13. In economics, an externality or spillover of an economic transaction is an impact on a party that is not directly involved in the transaction. In such a case, prices do not reflect the full costs or benefits in production or consumption of a product or service. A positive impact is called an _____ benefit, while a negative impact is called an _____ cost.

    a. ADTECH
    b. AMAX
    c. External
    d. ACNielsen

14. A supply chain is the system of organizations, people, technology, activities, information and resources involved in moving a product or service from _____ to customer. Supply chain activities transform natural resources, raw materials and components into a finished product that is delivered to the end customer. In sophisticated supply chain systems, used products may re-enter the supply chain at any point where residual value is recyclable.

    a. Rebate
    b. Supplier
    c. Product line extension
    d. Bringin' Home the Oil

15. _____ is a process by which products are designed with ease of assembly in mind. If a product contains fewer parts it will take less time to assemble, thereby reducing assembly costs. In addition, if the parts are provided with features which make it easier to grasp, move, orient and insert them, this will also reduce assembly time and assembly costs.

    a. Specification
    b. New product development
    c. Specification tree
    d. Design for assembly

16. _____ is systematic determination of merit, worth, and significance of something or someone using criteria against a set of standards. _____ often is used to characterize and appraise subjects of interest in a wide range of human enterprises, including the arts, criminal justice, foundations and non-profit organizations, government, health care, and other human services.

    Depending on the topic of interest, there are professional groups which look to the quality and rigor of the _____ process.

    a. AMAX
    b. Evaluation
    c. ACNielsen
    d. ADTECH

Chapter 11. Design for Manufacturing

17. A _____ is a set of exclusive rights granted by a State to an inventor or his assignee for a limited period of time in exchange for a disclosure of an invention.

The procedure for granting _____s, the requirements placed on the _____ee and the extent of the exclusive rights vary widely between countries according to national laws and international agreements. Typically, however, a _____ application must include one or more claims defining the invention which must be new, inventive, and useful or industrially applicable.

a. Foreign Corrupt Practices Act
b. Product liability
c. Reasonable person standard
d. Patent

Chapter 12. Prototyping

1. 'Speaking generally, properties are those physical quantities which directly describe the physical attributes of the system; _____s are those combinations of the properties which suffice to determine the response of the system. Properties can have all sorts of dimensions, depending upon the system being considered; _____s are dimensionless, or have the dimension of time or its reciprocal.'

   The term can also be used in engineering contexts, however, as it is typically used in the physical sciences.

   When the terms formal _____ and actual _____ are used, they generally correspond with the definitions used in computer science.

   a. Power III
   b. 180SearchAssistant
   c. 6-3-5 Brainwriting
   d. Parameter

2. Proof-of-Principle _____ This type of _____ is used to test some aspect of the intended design without attempting to exactly simulate the visual appearance, choice of materials or intended manufacturing process. Such _____s can be used to 'prove' out a potential design approach such as range of motion, mechanics, sensors, architecture, etc.
   a. 180SearchAssistant
   b. Power III
   c. 6-3-5 Brainwriting
   d. Prototype

3. The Program (or Project) Evaluation and Review Technique, commonly abbreviated _____, is a model for project management designed to analyze and represent the tasks involved in completing a given project.

   _____ is a method to analyze the involved tasks in completing a given project, especially the time needed to complete each task, and identifying the minimum time needed to complete the total project.

   This model was invented by Booz Allen Hamilton, Inc.

   a. 6-3-5 Brainwriting
   b. Power III
   c. 180SearchAssistant
   d. PERT

4. _____ is the automatic construction of physical objects using solid freeform fabrication. The first techniques for _____ became available in the late 1980s and were used to produce models and prototype parts. Today, they are used for a much wider range of applications and are even used to manufacture production quality parts in relatively small numbers.

a. Product management
b. Product lifecycle
c. Service life
d. Rapid prototyping

5. _____ in organizations and public policy is both the organizational process of creating and maintaining a plan; and the psychological process of thinking about the activities required to create a desired goal on some scale. As such, it is a fundamental property of intelligent behavior. This thought process is essential to the creation and refinement of a plan, or integration of it with other plans, that is, it combines forecasting of developments with the preparation of scenarios of how to react to them.
a. Power III
b. 180SearchAssistant
c. 6-3-5 Brainwriting
d. Planning

Chapter 13. Robust Design

1. 'Speaking generally, properties are those physical quantities which directly describe the physical attributes of the system; _____s are those combinations of the properties which suffice to determine the response of the system. Properties can have all sorts of dimensions, depending upon the system being considered; _____s are dimensionless, or have the dimension of time or its reciprocal.'

   The term can also be used in engineering contexts, however, as it is typically used in the physical sciences.

   When the terms formal _____ and actual _____ are used, they generally correspond with the definitions used in computer science.

   a. Power III
   b. 6-3-5 Brainwriting
   c. 180SearchAssistant
   d. Parameter

2. _____ is the imitation of some real thing, state of affairs, or process. The act of simulating something generally entails representing certain key characteristics or behaviors of a selected physical or abstract system.

   _____ is used in many contexts, including the modeling of natural systems or human systems in order to gain insight into their functioning.

   a. 6-3-5 Brainwriting
   b. 180SearchAssistant
   c. Power III
   d. Simulation

3. A personal and cultural _____ is a relative ethic _____, an assumption upon which implementation can be extrapolated. A _____ system is a set of consistent _____s and measures that is soo not true. A principle _____ is a foundation upon which other _____s and measures of integrity are based.
   a. Supreme Court of the United States
   b. Value
   c. Perceptual maps
   d. Package-on-Package

4. In mathematics, an _____, or central tendency of a data set refers to a measure of the 'middle' or 'expected' value of the data set. There are many different descriptive statistics that can be chosen as a measurement of the central tendency of the data items.

   An _____ is a single value that is meant to typify a list of values.

a. AMAX
b. ACNielsen
c. Average
d. ADTECH

5. In statistics, _____ has two related meanings:

- the arithmetic _____
- the expected value of a random variable, which is also called the population _____.

It is sometimes stated that the '_____' _____s average. This is incorrect if '_____' is taken in the specific sense of 'arithmetic _____' as there are different types of averages: the _____, median, and mode. For instance, average house prices almost always use the median value for the average. These three types of averages are all measures of locations.

a. Mean
b. Heteroskedastic
c. Confidence interval
d. Standard normal distribution

6. In descriptive statistics, the _____ is the length of the smallest interval which contains all the data. It is calculated by subtracting the smallest observation (sample minimum) from the greatest (sample maximum) and provides an indication of statistical dispersion.

It is measured in the same units as the data.

a. Just-In-Case
b. Range
c. Personalization
d. Japan Advertising Photographers' Association

7. In statistics, analysis of variance (_____) is a collection of statistical models, and their associated procedures, in which the observed variance is partitioned into components due to different explanatory variables. In its simplest form _____ gives a statistical test of whether the means of several groups are all equal, and therefore generalizes Student's two-sample t-test to more than two groups.

Chapter 13. Robust Design 51

There are three conceptual classes of such models:

1. Fixed-effects models assumes that the data came from normal populations which may differ only in their means. (Model 1)
2. Random effects models assume that the data describe a hierarchy of different populations whose differences are constrained by the hierarchy. (Model 2)
3. Mixed-effect models describe situations where both fixed and random effects are present. (Model 3)

In practice, there are several types of _____ depending on the number of treatments and the way they are applied to the subjects in the experiment:

- One-way _____ is used to test for differences among two or more independent groups. Typically, however, the one-way _____ is used to test for differences among at least three groups, since the two-group case can be covered by a T-test (Gossett, 1908.)

a. ACNielsen
b. ADTECH
c. AMAX
d. ANOVA

8. In statistics, _____ is a collection of statistical models, and their associated procedures, in which the observed variance is partitioned into components due to different explanatory variables. The initial techniques of the _____ were developed by the statistician and geneticist R. A. Fisher in the 1920s and 1930s, and is sometimes known as Fisher's ANOVA or Fisher's _____, due to the use of Fisher's F-distribution as part of the test of statistical significance.

There are three conceptual classes of such models:

1. Fixed-effects models assumes that the data came from normal populations which may differ only in their means. (Model 1)
2. Random effects models assume that the data describe a hierarchy of different populations whose differences are constrained by the hierarchy. (Model 2)
3. Mixed-effect models describe situations where both fixed and random effects are present. (Model 3)

In practice, there are several types of ANOVA depending on the number of treatments and the way they are applied to the subjects in the experiment:

- One-way ANOVA is used to test for differences among two or more independent groups. Typically, however, the One-way ANOVA is used to test for differences among at least three groups, since the two-group case can be covered by a T-test (Gossett, 1908.)

a. Analysis of variance
b. ACNielsen
c. Arithmetic mean
d. Interval estimation

9. In probability theory and statistics, the _____ of a random variable, probability distribution, or sample is a measure of statistical dispersion, averaging the squared distance of its possible values from the expected value (mean.) Whereas the mean is a way to describe the location of a distribution, the _____ is a way to capture its scale or degree of being spread out. The unit of _____ is the square of the unit of the original variable.

a. Correlation
b. Sample size
c. Standard deviation
d. Variance

10. A _____ is a set of exclusive rights granted by a State to an inventor or his assignee for a limited period of time in exchange for a disclosure of an invention.

The procedure for granting _____s, the requirements placed on the _____ee and the extent of the exclusive rights vary widely between countries according to national laws and international agreements. Typically, however, a _____ application must include one or more claims defining the invention which must be new, inventive, and useful or industrially applicable.

a. Product liability
b. Patent
c. Foreign Corrupt Practices Act
d. Reasonable person standard

Chapter 14. Patents and Intellectual Property

1. A _____ is a set of exclusive rights granted by a State to an inventor or his assignee for a limited period of time in exchange for a disclosure of an invention.

The procedure for granting _____s, the requirements placed on the _____ee and the extent of the exclusive rights vary widely between countries according to national laws and international agreements. Typically, however, a _____ application must include one or more claims defining the invention which must be new, inventive, and useful or industrially applicable.

   a. Reasonable person standard
   b. Foreign Corrupt Practices Act
   c. Product liability
   d. Patent

2. _____ is a form of intellectual property which gives the creator of an original work exclusive rights for a certain time period in relation to that work, including its publication, distribution and adaptation; after which time the work is said to enter the public domain. _____ applies to any expressible form of an idea or information that is substantive and discrete. Some jurisdictions also recognize 'moral rights' of the creator of a work, such as the right to be credited for the work.

   a. Reasonable person standard
   b. Collective mark
   c. Celler-Kefauver Act
   d. Copyright

3. _____ are legal property rights over creations of the mind, both artistic and commercial, and the corresponding fields of law. Under _____ law, owners are granted certain exclusive rights to a variety of intangible assets, such as musical, literary, and artistic works; ideas, discoveries and inventions; and words, phrases, symbols, and designs. Common types of _____ include copyrights, trademarks, patents, industrial design rights and trade secrets.

   a. Intellectual property
   b. Opinion leadership
   c. ACNielsen
   d. Elasticity

4. A _____ is a formula, practice, process, design, instrument, pattern by which a business can obtain an economic advantage over competitors or customers. In some jurisdictions, such secrets are referred to as 'confidential information' or 'classified information'.

The precise language by which a _____ is defined varies by jurisdiction (as do the particular types of information that are subject to _____ protection.)

Chapter 14. Patents and Intellectual Property

a. Priority right
b. CAN-SPAM
c. Trade secret
d. Federal Bureau of Investigation

5. A _____ or trade mark, identified by the symbols â„¢ (not yet registered) and Â® (registered) business organization or other legal entity to identify that the products and/or services to consumers with which the _____ appears originate from a unique source of origin, and to distinguish its products or services from those of other entities. A _____ is a type of intellectual property, and typically a name, word, phrase, logo, symbol, design, image, or a combination of these elements. There is also a range of non-conventional _____s comprising marks which do not fall into these standard categories.
   a. 180SearchAssistant
   b. Power III
   c. Risk management
   d. Trademark

6. An _____ is a person who creates or discovers a new method, form, device or other useful means. The word _____ comes form the latin verb invenire, invent-, to find. The system of patents was established to encourage _____s by granting limited-term, limited monopoly on inventions determined to be sufficiently novel, non-obvious, and useful.
   a. ACNielsen
   b. ADTECH
   c. AMAX
   d. Inventor

7. In economics, _____ is a measure of the relative satisfaction from consumption of various goods and services. Given this measure, one may speak meaningfully of increasing or decreasing _____, and thereby explain economic behavior in terms of attempts to increase one's _____. For illustrative purposes, changes in _____ are sometimes expressed in units called utils.
   a. AMAX
   b. ADTECH
   c. ACNielsen
   d. Utility

8. _____ is the state or fact of exclusive rights and control over property, which may be an object, land/real estate, or some other kind of property (like government-granted monopolies collectively referred to as intellectual property.) It is embodied in an _____ right also referred to as title.

_____ is the key building block in the development of the capitalist socio-economic system.

Chapter 14. Patents and Intellectual Property 55

   a. AMAX
   b. ACNielsen
   c. Ownership
   d. ADTECH

9. A _____ is a plan of action designed to achieve a particular goal.

   _____ is different from tactics. In military terms, tactics is concerned with the conduct of an engagement while _____ is concerned with how different engagements are linked.

   a. 6-3-5 Brainwriting
   b. 180SearchAssistant
   c. Strategy
   d. Power III

10. A _____ is an explicit set of requirements to be satisfied by a material, product, or service.

    In engineering, manufacturing, and business, it is vital for suppliers, purchasers, and users of materials, products, or services to understand and agree upon all requirements. A _____ is a type of a standard which is often referenced by a contract or procurement document.

    a. New product development
    b. Product development
    c. Product optimization
    d. Specification

11. An _____ is a document written by an examiner in a patent or trademark examination procedure and mailed to an applicant for a patent or trademark. The expression is used in many jurisdictions.

    In United States trademark law, an _____ is a rejection of an application to register a trademark issued by an examiner for the United States Patent and Trademark Office (USPTO.)

    a. Imperial Group v. Philip Morris
    b. Express warranty
    c. Office for Harmonization in the Internal Market
    d. Office action

Chapter 14. Patents and Intellectual Property

12. Once trademark rights are established in a particular jurisdiction, these rights are generally only enforceable in that jurisdiction, a quality which is sometimes known as territoriality. However, there is a range of international _____ and systems which facilitate the protection of trademarks in more than one jurisdiction

To avoid conflicts with earlier trademark rights, it is highly recommended to conduct trademark searches before the trademarks office (or 'trademarks registry') of a particular jurisdiction--e.g. US Patent and Trademark Office.

   a. Supreme Court of the United States
   b. Trademark laws
   c. Sigg bottles
   d. Self branding

13. The _____ is an agency in the United States Department of Commerce that issues patents to inventors and businesses for their inventions, and trademark registration for product and intellectual property identification.

The USPTO is currently based in Alexandria, Virginia, after a 2006 move from the Crystal City area of Arlington, Virginia. The offices under Patents and the Chief Information Officer that remained just outside the southern end of Crystal City completed moving to Randolph Square, a brand new building in Shirlington Village, on 27 April 2009.

   a. Access Commerce
   b. INVISTA
   c. United States Patent and Trademark Office
   d. Underwriters Laboratories

14. A personal and cultural _____ is a relative ethic _____, an assumption upon which implementation can be extrapolated. A _____ system is a set of consistent _____s and measures that is soo not true. A principle _____ is a foundation upon which other _____s and measures of integrity are based.
   a. Package-on-Package
   b. Perceptual maps
   c. Supreme Court of the United States
   d. Value

15. The verb _____ or grant _____ means to give permission. The noun _____ refers to that permission as well as to the document memorializing that permission. _____ may be granted by a party to another party as an element of an agreement between those parties.

a. 6-3-5 Brainwriting
b. Power III
c. 180SearchAssistant
d. License

Chapter 15. Product Development Economics

1. _____s is the social science that studies the production, distribution, and consumption of goods and services. The term _____s comes from the Ancient Greek οἰκονομία from οἶκος (oikos, 'house') + νόμος (nomos, 'custom' or 'law'), hence 'rules of the house(hold)'. Current _____ models developed out of the broader field of political economy in the late 19th century, owing to a desire to use an empirical approach more akin to the physical sciences.
   a. Economic
   b. ADTECH
   c. Industrial organization
   d. ACNielsen

2. In business and engineering, new _____ is the term used to describe the complete process of bringing a new product or service to market. There are two parallel paths involved in the Nproduct development process: one involves the idea generation, product design, and detail engineering; the other involves market research and marketing analysis. Companies typically see new _____ as the first stage in generating and commercializing new products within the overall strategic process of product life cycle management used to maintain or grow their market share.
   a. Specification tree
   b. New product screening
   c. New product development
   d. Product development

3. A _____ attribute is one that exists in a range of magnitudes, and can therefore be measured. Measurements of any particular _____ property are expressed as a specific quantity, referred to as a unit, multiplied by a number. Examples of physical quantities are distance, mass, and time.
   a. Lifestyle city
   b. Dolly Dimples
   c. BeyondROI
   d. Quantitative

4. A personal and cultural _____ is a relative ethic _____, an assumption upon which implementation can be extrapolated. A _____ system is a set of consistent _____s and measures that is soo not true. A principle _____ is a foundation upon which other _____s and measures of integrity are based.
   a. Package-on-Package
   b. Supreme Court of the United States
   c. Value
   d. Perceptual maps

5. _____ is the process of estimation in unknown situations. Prediction is a similar, but more general term. Both can refer to estimation of time series, cross-sectional or longitudinal data.

Chapter 15. Product Development Economics

a. Forecasting
b. 6-3-5 Brainwriting
c. Power III
d. 180SearchAssistant

6. In economics, an externality or spillover of an economic transaction is an impact on a party that is not directly involved in the transaction. In such a case, prices do not reflect the full costs or benefits in production or consumption of a product or service. A positive impact is called an _____ benefit, while a negative impact is called an _____ cost.
   a. External
   b. ACNielsen
   c. AMAX
   d. ADTECH

7. In economics, business, retail, and accounting, a _____ is the value of money that has been used up to produce something, and hence is not available for use anymore. In economics, a _____ is an alternative that is given up as a result of a decision. In business, the _____ may be one of acquisition, in which case the amount of money expended to acquire it is counted as _____.
   a. Fixed costs
   b. Transaction cost
   c. Cost
   d. Variable cost

8. In statistics, an _____ is a term in a statistical model added when the effect of two or more variables is not simply additive. Such a term reflects that the effect of one variable depends on the values of one or more other variables.

Thus, for a response Y and two variables x_1 and x_2 an additive model would be:

$$Y = ax_1 + bx_2 + \text{error}$$

In contrast to this,

$$Y = ax_1 + bx_2 + c(x_1 \times x_2) + \text{error},$$

is an example of a model with an _____ between variables x_1 and x_2 ('error' refers to the random variable whose value by which y differs from the expected value of y.)

Chapter 15. Product Development Economics

   a. ADTECH
   b. Interaction
   c. ACNielsen
   d. AMAX

9. _____ is a measure of the strength of a brand, product, service relative to competitive offerings. There is often a geographic element to the competitive landscape. In defining _____, you must see to what extent a product, brand, or firm controls a product category in a given geographic area.
   a. Productivity
   b. Market dominance
   c. Market system
   d. Discretionary spending

10. A supply chain is the system of organizations, people, technology, activities, information and resources involved in moving a product or service from _____ to customer. Supply chain activities transform natural resources, raw materials and components into a finished product that is delivered to the end customer. In sophisticated supply chain systems, used products may re-enter the supply chain at any point where residual value is recyclable.
    a. Product line extension
    b. Rebate
    c. Supplier
    d. Bringin' Home the Oil

11. _____ refers to 'controlling human or societal behaviour by rules or restrictions.' _____ can take many forms: legal restrictions promulgated by a government authority, self-_____, social _____, co-_____ and market _____. One can consider _____ as actions of conduct imposing sanctions (such as a fine.) This action of administrative law, or implementing regulatory law, may be contrasted with statutory or case law.
    a. Regulation
    b. Rule of four
    c. CAN-SPAM
    d. Non-conventional trademark

12. _____ is a rivalry between individuals, groups, nations for territory, a niche, or allocation of resources. It arises whenever two or more parties strive for a goal which cannot be shared. _____ occurs naturally between living organisms which co-exist in the same environment.

a. Price competition
b. Non-price competition
c. Price fixing
d. Competition

13. _____ is anything that is generally accepted as payment for goods and services and repayment of debts. The main uses of _____ are as a medium of exchange, a unit of account, and a store of value. Some authors explicitly require _____ to be a standard of deferred payment.
a. Microeconomics
b. Leading indicator
c. Law of supply
d. Money

14. _____ is a fee paid on borrowed assets. It is the price paid for the use of borrowed money, or, money earned by deposited funds. Assets that are sometimes lent with _____ include money, shares, consumer goods through hire purchase, major assets such as aircraft, and even entire factories in finance lease arrangements.
a. Interest
b. AMAX
c. ADTECH
d. ACNielsen

15. _____ is a concept that denotes the precise probability of specific eventualities. Technically, the notion of _____ is independent from the notion of value and, as such, eventualities may have both beneficial and adverse consequences. However, in general usage the convention is to focus only on potential negative impact to some characteristic of value that may arise from a future event.
a. Power III
b. Risk
c. 6-3-5 Brainwriting
d. 180SearchAssistant

16.

_____ is a systematic method to improve the 'value' of goods or products and services by using an examination of function. Value, as defined, is the ratio of function to cost. Value can therefore be increased by either improving the function or reducing the cost.

Chapter 15. Product Development Economics

a. Power III
b. Value engineering
c. 180SearchAssistant
d. Productivity

17. _____ is the risk that the value of an investment will decrease due to moves in market factors. The four standard _____ factors are:

- Equity risk, the risk that stock prices will change.
- Interest rate risk, the risk that interest rates will change.
- Currency risk, the risk that foreign exchange rates will change.
- Commodity risk, the risk that commodity prices (e.g. grains, metals) will change.

As with other forms of risk, _____ may be measured in a number of ways. Traditionally, this is done using a Value at Risk methodology. Value at risk is well established as a risk management technique, but it contains a number of limiting assumptions that constrain its accuracy.

a. 6-3-5 Brainwriting
b. 180SearchAssistant
c. Power III
d. Market risk

18. In finance, an _____ is a contract between a buyer and a seller that gives the buyer the right--but not the obligation-- to buy or to sell a particular asset (the underlying asset) at a later day at an agreed price. In return for granting the _____, the seller collects a payment (the premium) from the buyer. A call _____ gives the buyer the right to buy the underlying asset; a put _____ gives the buyer of the _____ the right to sell the underlying asset.

a. Option
b. AMAX
c. ADTECH
d. ACNielsen

Chapter 16. Managing Projects

1. The Program (or Project) Evaluation and Review Technique, commonly abbreviated _____, is a model for project management designed to analyze and represent the tasks involved in completing a given project.

   _____ is a method to analyze the involved tasks in completing a given project, especially the time needed to complete each task, and identifying the minimum time needed to complete the total project.

   This model was invented by Booz Allen Hamilton, Inc.

   a. Power III
   b. PERT
   c. 180SearchAssistant
   d. 6-3-5 Brainwriting

2. _____ is part of project management, which relates to the use of schedules such as Gantt charts to plan and subsequently report progress within the project environment.

   Initially, the project scope is defined and the appropriate methods for completing the project are determined. Following this step, the durations for the various tasks necessary to complete the work are listed and grouped into a work breakdown structure.

   a. 180SearchAssistant
   b. Power III
   c. Product breakdown structure
   d. Project planning

3. _____ in organizations and public policy is both the organizational process of creating and maintaining a plan; and the psychological process of thinking about the activities required to create a desired goal on some scale. As such, it is a fundamental property of intelligent behavior. This thought process is essential to the creation and refinement of a plan, or integration of it with other plans, that is, it combines forecasting of developments with the preparation of scenarios of how to react to them.
   a. 180SearchAssistant
   b. Planning
   c. Power III
   d. 6-3-5 Brainwriting

4. In business and engineering, new _____ is the term used to describe the complete process of bringing a new product or service to market. There are two parallel paths involved in the Nproduct development process: one involves the idea generation, product design, and detail engineering; the other involves market research and marketing analysis. Companies typically see new _____ as the first stage in generating and commercializing new products within the overall strategic process of product life cycle management used to maintain or grow their market share.

Chapter 16. Managing Projects

   a. New product development
   b. New product screening
   c. Specification tree
   d. Product development

5. A _____ is a type of bar chart that illustrates a project schedule. A _____ illustrates the start and finish dates of the terminal elements and summary elements of a project. Terminal elements and summary elements comprise the work breakdown structure of the project.
   a. Gantt chart
   b. 180SearchAssistant
   c. Power III
   d. 6-3-5 Brainwriting

6. _____ generally refers to a list of all planned expenses and revenues. It is a plan for saving and spending. A _____ is an important concept in microeconomics, which uses a _____ line to illustrate the trade-offs between two or more goods.
   a. Power III
   b. 6-3-5 Brainwriting
   c. 180SearchAssistant
   d. Budget

7. In economics, business, retail, and accounting, a _____ is the value of money that has been used up to produce something, and hence is not available for use anymore. In economics, a _____ is an alternative that is given up as a result of a decision. In business, the _____ may be one of acquisition, in which case the amount of money expended to acquire it is counted as _____.
   a. Variable cost
   b. Transaction cost
   c. Fixed costs
   d. Cost

8. _____ is a concept that denotes the precise probability of specific eventualities. Technically, the notion of _____ is independent from the notion of value and, as such, eventualities may have both beneficial and adverse consequences. However, in general usage the convention is to focus only on potential negative impact to some characteristic of value that may arise from a future event.

Chapter 16. Managing Projects

a. Risk
b. Power III
c. 180SearchAssistant
d. 6-3-5 Brainwriting

9. _____ is the process of comparing the cost, cycle time, productivity, or quality of a specific process or method to another that is widely considered to be an industry standard or best practice. The result is often a business case for making changes in order to make improvements. The term _____ was first used by cobblers to measure ones feet for shoes.
   a. Strategic group
   b. Switching cost
   c. Business strategy
   d. Benchmarking

10. _____ is a technique used in propaganda and advertising. Also known as association, this is a technique of projecting positive or negative qualities (praise or blame) of a person, entity, object, or value (an individual, group, organization, nation, patriotism, etc.) to another in order to make the second more acceptable or to discredit it.
    a. Supplier
    b. Sexism,
    c. Micro ads
    d. Transfer

11. _____ is subcontracting a process, such as product design or manufacturing, to a third-party company. The decision to outsource is often made in the interest of lowering cost or making better use of time and energy costs, redirecting or conserving energy directed at the competencies of a particular business, or to make more efficient use of land, labor, capital, (information) technology and resources. _____ became part of the business lexicon during the 1980s.
    a. In-house
    b. Intangible assets
    c. ACNielsen
    d. Outsourcing

12. In economics and sociology, an _____ is any factor (financial or non-financial) that enables or motivates a particular course of action, or counts as a reason for preferring one choice to the alternatives. It is an expectation that encourages people to behave in a certain way. Since human beings are purposeful creatures, the study of _____ structures is central to the study of all economic activity (both in terms of individual decision-making and in terms of co-operation and competition within a larger institutional structure.)

a. Incentive
b. ADTECH
c. AMAX
d. ACNielsen

13. _____ is a term used by project managers and project management (PM) organizations to describe methods for analyzing and collectively managing a group of current or proposed projects based on numerous key characteristics. The fundamental objective of the _____ process is to determine the optimal mix and sequencing of proposed projects to best achieve the organization's overall goals - typically expressed in terms of hard economic measures, business strategy goals, or technical strategy goals - while honoring constraints imposed by management or external real-world factors. Typical attributes of projects being analyzed in a _____ process include each project's total expected cost, consumption of scarce resources (human or otherwise) expected timeline and schedule of investment, expected nature, magnitude and timing of benefits to be realized, and relationship or inter-dependencies with other projects in the portfolio.

   a. Pop-up ads
   b. Project Portfolio Management
   c. Power III
   d. Customer intelligence

14. _____ is systematic determination of merit, worth, and significance of something or someone using criteria against a set of standards. _____ often is used to characterize and appraise subjects of interest in a wide range of human enterprises, including the arts, criminal justice, foundations and non-profit organizations, government, health care, and other human services.

Depending on the topic of interest, there are professional groups which look to the quality and rigor of the _____ process.

   a. AMAX
   b. ACNielsen
   c. Evaluation
   d. ADTECH

15. Human beings are also considered to be _____ because they have the ability to change raw materials into valuable _____. The term Human _____ can also be defined as the skills, energies, talents, abilities and knowledge that are used for the production of goods or the rendering of services. While taking into account human beings as _____, the following things have to be kept in mind:

   - The size of the population
   - The capabilities of the individuals in that population

Many _____ cannot be consumed in their original form. They have to be processed in order to change them into more usable commodities.

a. Power III
b. 180SearchAssistant
c. 6-3-5 Brainwriting
d. Resources

Chapter 1
1. b 2. b 3. d 4. b 5. a 6. d 7. b 8. c

Chapter 2
1. b 2. a 3. d 4. b 5. d 6. d 7. d 8. a 9. a 10. a
11. c 12. d 13. b 14. d 15. a 16. d

Chapter 3
1. d 2. c 3. c 4. d 5. a 6. d 7. d 8. a 9. d 10. d
11. b 12. c 13. b 14. d 15. d 16. c 17. a 18. c

Chapter 4
1. d 2. d 3. b 4. d 5. d 6. c 7. c 8. d 9. b 10. d
11. d

Chapter 5
1. d 2. a 3. b 4. d 5. b 6. c 7. d 8. a 9. b 10. d
11. d 12. d 13. d 14. d 15. a 16. b 17. c 18. d 19. b 20. d
21. d

Chapter 6
1. b 2. d 3. d 4. c 5. d 6. d 7. a 8. a 9. d 10. d
11. d 12. a

Chapter 7
1. c 2. b 3. b 4. b 5. b 6. a 7. b 8. c

Chapter 8
1. a 2. b 3. a 4. d 5. d 6. b 7. d 8. d 9. d 10. d
11. b 12. b 13. d

Chapter 9
1. d 2. c 3. d 4. d 5. d 6. d 7. d 8. d 9. c

Chapter 10
1. a 2. d 3. c 4. d 5. c 6. a 7. d 8. d 9. b 10. d
11. d 12. d 13. c 14. d

Chapter 11
1. d 2. c 3. b 4. d 5. b 6. d 7. d 8. d 9. c 10. d
11. b 12. d 13. c 14. b 15. d 16. b 17. d

Chapter 12
1. d 2. d 3. d 4. d 5. d

ANSWER KEY

Chapter 13
1. d   2. d   3. b   4. c   5. a   6. b   7. d   8. a   9. d   10. b

Chapter 14
1. d   2. d   3. a   4. c   5. d   6. d   7. d   8. c   9. c   10. d
11. d   12. b   13. c   14. d   15. d

Chapter 15
1. a   2. d   3. d   4. c   5. a   6. a   7. c   8. b   9. b   10. c
11. a   12. d   13. d   14. a   15. b   16. b   17. d   18. a

Chapter 16
1. b   2. d   3. b   4. d   5. a   6. d   7. d   8. a   9. d   10. d
11. d   12. a   13. b   14. c   15. d

www.ingramcontent.com/pod-product-compliance
Lightning Source LLC
Chambersburg PA
CBHW081850230426
43669CB00018B/2892